An

C RT

Susi

Heinemann
LIBRARY

First published in Great Britain by Heinemann Library
Halley Court, Jordan Hill, Oxford OX2 8EJ
a division of Reed Educational and Professional Publishing Ltd

OXFORD FLORENCE PRAGUE MADRID ATHENS
MELBOURNE AUCKLAND KUALA LUMPUR SINGAPORE TOKYO
IBADAN NAIROBI KAMPALA JOHANNESBURG GABORONE
PORTSMOUTH NH CHICAGO MEXICO CITY SAO PAULO

Produced by Plum Creative
Illustrations by Oxford Illustrators
Printed in Hong Kong / China

01 00 99 98 97
10 9 8 7 6 5 4 3 2 1

ISBN 0 431 05627 7 (HB) ISBN 0 431 05606 4 (PB)

British Library Cataloguing in Publication Data
Hodge, Susie
    Ancient Greek art. – (Art in history)
    1. Art, Greek – Juvenile literature
    2. Art, Ancient – Greece – Juvenile literature
    I. Title
    709.3'8

Acknowledgements
The Publishers would like to thank the following for permission to reproduce photographs:
cover photo: The Bridgeman Art Library; Museo Archaeologico, Florence
other illustrations: AKG photo p.10, Metropolitan Museum of Art, NY p.14; Ancient Art & Architecture Collection, R. Sheridan pp.7, 8, 9, 12, 15, 19 (both), 28; Bridgeman Art Library, British Museum pp.13, 21, House of Masks, Delos, Greece p.16, K & B News Foto p.29, Museo & Gallerie Nazionali di Capodimonte, Naples p.17, National Archaeological Museum, Athens p.20, Vatican Museums & Galleries p.5, Peter Willi p.18; British Museum, London p.23; Corbis, W. Kaehler p.4, M. Nicholson p.27, G. D. Orti p.6; C. M. Dixon pp.11, 25; B. O. Giraudon p.26; Michael Holford p.24; Werner Forman Archive, British Museum p.22

Our thanks to Paul Flux and Jane Shuter for their comments in the preparation of this book.

Every effort to contact copyright holders of any material reproduced in this book. Any omissions will be rectified in subsequent printings if notice is given to the Publisher.

Cover picture: Two Amazons in combat with a greek tarquinia, about 400BC, fresco.
According to ancient Greek legend, Amazons were a race of warrior-women who lived on the shores of the Black Sea. Near the end of the end of the mythical Trojan War, the Amazons helped the Trojans to fight the Greeks. Ancient Greek artists painted and carved many pictures telling stories of Amazons and Greeks fighting. In the wall-painting on the cover, two Amazons are attacking a Greek soldier. The picture shows plenty of action. You can tell that real people have posed for the artist (or artists - usually several worked on one painting) to copy. Although the bright colours of the paint have faded with time, you can still see the clothes and armour clearly. Ancient Greek artists were beginning to use shading to make flat images look three-dimensional.

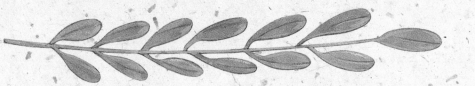

CONTENTS

WHO WERE THE ANCIENT GREEKS?

The earliest evidence we have of Greek culture is on the island of Crete. From about 3000BC to 1380BC, the Minoan people on the island of Crete farmed, built palaces and towns, and developed their own artistic style.

From about 2000BC, the Mycenaeans on the Greek mainland developed their own civilization. They traded with and fought against the Minoans and were influenced by Minoan art.

Dolphin Fresco, Knossos in Crete, about 1580BC, **fresco**.

The walls of Minoan palaces were richly decorated. These leaping dolphins are from the Queen's Room in the palace of the legendary King Minos.

Four periods

After the Mycenaeans, Greek art is usually divided into four main periods:

Geometric (1100–700BC) **Archaic** (700–500BC)
Classical (500–323BC) **Hellenistic** (323–100BC).

The most famous is the Classical period. It was the period when Greek art was at its best.

City states

Ancient Greece was made up of islands and two separate pieces of mainland that were covered with mountains. It was difficult to travel and hard to think of these places as being part of the same country. Early Greeks did not consider themselves Greek at all.

Greek civilization developed as many city states. Each was based on a city that controlled the farmland and villages around it. City states had different laws and ways of doing things. But they were united by one language.

Different city states were powerful at different times. Sometimes they fought each other and sometimes they joined forces. They were all united against the Persian invasion in 490BC. But after they had defeated the Persians they fought each other again.

Alexander the Great

From 336BC onwards, Alexander the Great united the city states so they could conquer the Persian Empire. But when he died Greece split up again. Weakened by being split up, Greece was gradually conquered by the Romans.

*Achilles and Ajax Playing Draughts, Exekias, about 540BC, 58 cm, **black-figure style** vase.*

Greek pottery was beautifully made. Even if they were only made to hold wine or oil, pots were called vases. Artists painted stories on them. This is a story from a Greek myth. The faces are painted in profile but the eyes are seen from the front.

MATERIALS AND METHODS

Mycenaean artists usually worked for the king. They trained as **apprentices** from a young age and worked together in workshops. Much of their work was traded for goods from other countries.

Later, art and craft skills were passed down through the family. Boys learned skills by helping their father, and his workmen and slaves. Few women were artists. Each workshop specialized in a particular kind of art or craft, such as stone carving or wall painting. Usually fewer than ten men worked in one workshop.

How artists were treated

At first, artists were seen as unimportant, common workmen because their hands got dirty when they worked. But by about 480BC art had become important. **Architects**, painters and sculptors were seen as skilled craftsmen, worthy of respect.

By the 5th century BC, the city states (such as Athens) were settled enough to devote time to art. Artists developed their skills to produce more lifelike work.

*Discus Thrower, Myron, about 450BC, 1.25 m, originally **bronze**.*

*Myron worked in the early **Classical period**. He liked to show movement frozen in time. This athlete is caught just as he is about to throw the discus. Sport was important in many Greek city states, and is often shown in statues and on painted vases.*

Artists' equipment

Greek artists painted on walls, wood or **marble** panels, **terracotta** slabs and sometimes pieces of ivory, leather, **parchment**, papyrus or linen. Wood was the most common choice. It was given a white undercoat first. Brushes and pens were made from reeds. Painters used **tempera** and **fresco** on walls.

They used tempera and **encaustic** on wood or marble.

The usual materials for sculpture were marble and bronze. **Limestone**, terracotta and wood were occasionally used, and sometimes gold and ivory with a wooden centre. Solid gold and silver were used for very special sculptures.

*Blacksmiths working at a furnace, about 580BC, **black-figure style** tile on yellow and white background, terracotta.*

Blacksmiths made metal tools that were used by many other Greek craftsmen and artists. Here, you can see the tools around them that they were making. The men are shown from the side, which was the accepted way to paint people at that time.

SIGNS AND SYMBOLS

The first Greek alphabet was made in about 700BC, at the start of the **Archaic period**. The Greeks developed it from earlier Phoenician writing which used symbols to represent sounds. Phoenician writing was read from right to left.

Two hundred years later, the Greeks changed it to read from left to right as we do today. They added new symbols to form an alphabet (this word comes from the first two letters – α or alpha and β or beta) of 24 letters. A written language meant that the Greeks could pass on ideas and information more easily.

Geometric period

After about 1100BC, Greek artists replaced the flowing Mycenaean patterns with lines and angles. People were shown as symbols (circles, rectangles and triangles). They were not shown as realistic images.

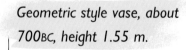

Geometric style vase, about 700BC, height 1.55 m.

This huge amphora (tall vase with two handles) was used for storing wine or oil. The geometric patterns show simplified people and 'key' shapes. You can see how the patterns resemble the writing that the Greeks developed.

α β χ δ ε φ γ η ι φ κ λ μ

How symbols developed

Ancient Greek artists drew a trident as a symbol of lightning, or a thunderbolt, coming from the thunderclouds to earth. They developed many more symbols, like the owl which became a symbol of Athena, and later Athens. Athenian coins were made with owls on one side. Today we use many of the ancient Greeks' symbols in horoscopes.

ν ο π θ ρ σ τ υ ϖ ω ξ ψ ζ

*Departure of Triptolemos, Makron, about 480BC, height 21 cm, **red-figure style** vase.*

*The Greeks told stories in pictures too. This vase, from the beginning of the **Classical Period**, shows the god Triptolemos, holding stalks of corn and a dish and sitting on a wheeled throne with wings. Persephone stands in front of him with a torch and a jug. Two other goddesses stand behind them. Triptolemos is about to take the corn to earth to teach humans how to grow crops.*

Written in stone

Much of what we know about the ancient Greeks comes from reading the inscriptions that they carved in stone. As time passed, more writing was done on **parchment** or other paper-like substances where a pen and ink could be used. This was much quicker than carving.

The writings of Greek historians, philosophers, poets and playwrights have taught us a great deal about how people lived and thought.

MISSING PICTURES

Why are there so many pots and statues? Why are there so few Greek paintings? How do we know that paintings existed? Well, we know that the Greeks produced beautiful paintings, particularly during the **Archaic**, **Classical** and **Hellenistic periods**, for these reasons:

• Ancient writers described them.
• Some fragments have survived.
• The Romans copied them later on.
• Vases which survived show the skills of painters.

The dry climate of the desert preserved many Egyptian paintings. But the Greek climate can be damp. Damp air destroys paintings and decays wood. Many Greek paintings were also destroyed when fighting between city states led to fires in the cities.

*Head of a Woman, 1300BC, **fresco**.*

*This fragment of a painting comes from a **frieze** that was inside a Greek palace. The woman's dress and the style of the painting come from Minoan times, but her face is Mycenaean. She is painted in profile, with her eye shown from the front. The paint has faded but you can see how flat, yet decorative early paintings were. Composition, or layout, was more important than being realistic.*

*Sacrifice with Musicians, Corinth in Greece, about 520–500BC, **tempera** on wood panel.*

This painting still makes the people look flat and shows them from the side, but now artists were beginning to paint folds in clothes and to put one person behind another to show three-dimensional space. In this painting, as in ancient Egyptian art, boys and men are painted with darker skin than girls and women.

Colour and decoration

Paintings were often used to decorate buildings. At first all paintings looked flat. The artists did not try to make anything look rounded or real. This is true of Minoan and Mycenaean art. But by studying real people, some Greek artists discovered how to make figures look lifelike. By the 5th century BC bright colours were still used, but with light and shade. This gave a three-dimensional effect. Atmosphere and moods were also created.

Paint palette

Paint colours were limited to what could be produced naturally. Brown, reds and yellow came from earth, rocks and clay; white came from chalk; black from soot; blue came from a kind of glass; green came from copper; and purple from a special seashell. **Pigments** were mixed with egg white to make a paste for painting.

POTTERY PICTURES

Decorating a pot is different to painting a picture on a flat surface. Some parts of a pot curve away from the viewer. The pot shape makes an oddly shaped frame. So Greek artists skilfully adjusted their designs to fit.

*Birth of Athena, about 400BC, **red-figure style** vase.*

In Greek legend, the god Hephaistos made a special axe. When it was time for Athena to be born, Hephaistos used the axe to cut Zeus's head open and Athena emerged. Even when the pictures of that story become distorted on the vase shape, they are clearly balanced and decorative.

Vase shapes

Greek pots were so well made that thousands of pieces have survived. They were strong and practical but also skilfully painted. Different shaped vases had different uses. For example, amphorae were used for storing wine. Kraters were for holding wine and water.

Black-figure style

Artists painted patterns and pictures on red-clay pots, with a mixture of clay, water and wood ash. They scratched details into the clay with a pointed tool and left the background red. They began firing the pot in the kiln — a special hot oven to bake clay. Then all the openings in the kiln were closed. The lack of air made the pot turn black. When air was let in again, the painted parts stayed black and the rest of the pot turned red.

Red-figure style

In about 510BC the red-figure style took over. The method was the same as the **black-figure style**, but this time the background was black and the figures appeared red. Details were outlined in black, using a fine brush. Curves are easier to draw with a brush than a scratching tool, so red-figure vases are more expressive.

Make a Greek tile

Materials:
self-hardening clay   water
carving and cutting tools brushes
paints   PVA glue.

1 Warm some clay in your hands. Shape it into a tile by rolling, pressing and cutting.

2 Smooth the clay with a little water and carve a picture using a stick. Leave it to dry.

3 Mix paint with some PVA glue and paint your tile brightly.

Wine vase, Athens in Greece, about 500BC, black-figure style vase, ceramic.

This large amphora was made for a special procession that went to the Parthenon every four years to make an offering to the goddess Athena. Because the horses are rearing and the man is leaning forward in the chariot, the picture appears to be moving as it curves around the vase.

THE BREAK WITH TRADITION

Ancient Greek art developed over centuries, from the Minoans in 5000BC onwards. It also borrowed artistic ideas from other people that it came into contact with through trade.

At first, art was mainly to do with the afterlife. Painted tombs, statues and masks were to help the dead travel to the next world. This was similar to the Egyptians, one of the peoples the Greeks traded with.

*Wedding Procession, by Exekias, Athens in Greece, about 540BC, height 47 cm, **black-figure style** vase, ceramic.*

Exekias was one of the finest black-figure painters of Athens. This amphora includes some white and red paint to show details, although the picture follows ancient rules making the humans and animals look as simple as possible. Soon, the rules were forgotten as it became important to make everything look lifelike.

Egyptian rules

Many artists working in the **Geometric period** followed Egyptian rules. They did not paint or carve what they saw. They just showed what they knew to be there. For example, people made from simple shapes were recognizable but not realistic.

Archaic art

During the **Archaic period**, artists began producing temples and huge statues. The statues were again made according to ancient Egyptian rules. They look stiff and awkward. But on pots, more flowing **red-figure** painting took over from black-figure painting.

The golden age

Early in 500BC many artists, especially those in more settled city states like Athens, began to produce more lifelike art. They tried to make flat pictures look three-dimensional and stiff sculptures look natural. They became fascinated with **proportion** and **symmetry**.

Art thrived when city states were not at war with each other. Painters began using shadows and highlights. They also studied perspective (how to make things look far away) and foreshortening (how to make thing look close). They invented **optical illusion** by making flat pictures look real. They painted objects from different angles, too.

Changing art

By the **Hellenistic period** art was less connected with religion. Artists became more interested in the problems of creating beautiful images. Writers took more interest in art. Art had changed a lot.

Tombstone of Hegeso, about 420BC, stone.

*This carved picture is called a **relief**. Hegeso sits, selecting jewellery from her servant. See how realistic the women and their draped clothes look.*

MARVELLOUS MOSAICS

The Greeks developed many ways of making pictures. They made **frescoes**, **murals**, **reliefs**, **encaustic** and mosaics.

Mosaics are patterns made with hundreds of tiny squares of coloured glass, pebbles, gold or **marble**. Ancient Greek artists invented mosaic pictures. At first they were only made on floors, but later wall mosaics were made as well.

How mosaics were made

Stones, glass or gold were collected and cut into square or diamond shapes. These were called tessellated mosaics. Glass was used sparingly on floors, but generously on walls. The mosaics were sorted into groups of colours. A kind of cement mixture was spread on the floor or wall.

Artists followed a previously drawn plan, showing them where to put the colours. They pushed in the mosaics while the cement was still wet. By 300BC, artists were so good at mosaics they could cut tiny pieces of brilliant colours and produce particularly detailed pictures.

Dionysus Riding a Leopard, from the House of Masks, Delos in Greece, about AD180, mosaic.

Mosaics are often colourful, detailed and shiny. Because the cement was strong, many ancient Greek mosaics have remained clear. Like most other Greek art of the time, the subject of this picture is animals, monsters and myths, with measured patterns around them.

The Alexander Mosaic, from Naples in Italy, 1st century BC, 3.42 m, mosaic. (From a copy of a painting by Philoxenos, about 300BC)

Alexander the Great conquered a vast empire, stretching from Egypt to India. This famous but damaged wall mosaic shows his victory over the Persians. It is a Roman copy of a Greek painting made during the late 4th century BC. The Romans borrowed the use of mosaics from the Greeks. This mosaic is skilfully done, using foreshortening and perspective. It contains only four colours: red, brown, black and white.

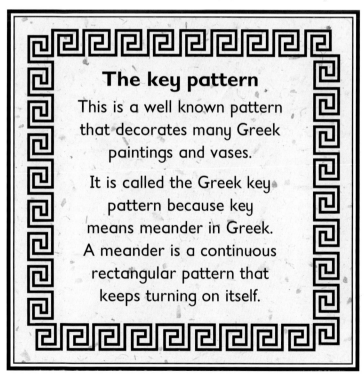

The key pattern

This is a well known pattern that decorates many Greek paintings and vases.

It is called the Greek key pattern because key means meander in Greek. A meander is a continuous rectangular pattern that keeps turning on itself.

Glittering walls

Floor mosaics had to be smooth and flat, but wall mosaics could be more uneven. Light reflected off the shiny surfaces, making the picture glitter.

THE DEVELOPMENT OF SCULPTURE

Sculptors made statues to decorate temples, tombs, monuments and homes. They used a number of techniques and various materials. Although most originals have been lost, many Roman copies of Greek statues have survived.

Classical sculpture

By **Classical** times, sculptors could show the body in a relaxed-looking, lifelike way. Legs placed apart showed movement, while faces looked gentle and smiling. Flowing clothes were gracefully folded, or bodies were naked with every muscle showing.

*Venus di Milo, from Milo in Greece, about 130BC, 2.02 m, **marble**.*

*This statue is of Aphrodite, the goddess of love (Venus is her Roman name). It is famous because she is both Classical and **Hellenistic**. She has perfect **proportions**, serene features, flowing drapery and a curved body. No one is sure what her arms were like as they were broken off long ago. Some say she held a mirror, a crown, an apple or a dove. What do you think?*

Stone statues

Large blocks of stone were difficult to move, so rough shapes of statues were cut in the quarry. Details were carved later in workshops. Statues were painted with bright colours, most of which have been worn away. Glass or coloured stones were sometimes used for eyes.

Expression and proportion

As sculptors of the Classical period became more skilled, they began producing portraits of real people. Even so, it was important to give them perfect-looking bodies.

Later, during the Hellenistic period, artists became interested in truthful images. Even old or deformed people were represented.

Lost wax sculptures

First a clay core was made and pins stuck in it. Wax was moulded around it to make the shape of the statue. This was coated with more clay, leaving a hole in the bottom. It was heated so the wax melted and ran out, leaving a space between the two lots of clay. Molten **bronze** was poured into the hole. When it had set, the clay was removed leaving the finished statue.

Artemision Horse and Jockey, Athens in Greece, 3rd to 2nd century BC, bronze.

This racehorse and boy rider in action are so realistic that they look as if they are about to gallop away! This is not a real portrait but was made to show how jockeys rode bare-back and were usually servants, but racehorses were noble expensive animals. Notice the boy's tousled hair. Hellenistic sculptors made their work as lifelike as possible.

ART FOR THE GODS

Until the **Hellenistic period**, Greek artists often included gods and goddesses in their work. The Greeks believed in many gods and goddesses and had hundreds of stories about them. Gods and goddesses were said to control all aspects of life and death, and had the same emotions as humans. They could come to earth in a human shape if they wished, and change people's lives.

Art and prayer

Greek temples, statues and **friezes** were dedicated to the gods. Vase paintings show soldiers pouring wine into a bowl on the altar or on to the ground before leaving home. They are asking the gods for victory in battle. People prayed to statues of the gods and made sacrifices to them. Statues were brightly painted or made of precious materials. Many were huge and by the **Classical period** they were incredibly lifelike.

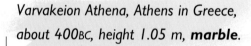

*Varvakeion Athena, Athens in Greece, about 400BC, height 1.05 m, **marble**.*

*Athena was the patron goddess of the city of Athens and also the goddess of wisdom and warfare. This marble statue was copied from a much larger one that stood in the **Parthenon** (see opposite). On Athena's helmet are flying horses and a sphinx (half-human, half-beast). The goddess's gently flowing hair, yet strong facial features were signs of Greek beauty.*

The Great Goddess Athena

A twelve metre high statue of the goddess Athena originally stood in the Parthenon. Covered in gold, ivory and coloured stones, she was made by a famous Greek sculptor called Phidias who created powerful yet graceful sculptures. The statue of Athena must have looked startling to people entering the temple.

Friezes

Phidias also carved a frieze on the Parthenon. The frieze showed scenes from the Great Panathanaea festival. This was when the people of the city paid tribute to Athena. No one knows who chose the subjects for the sculptures in Greek temples, but they show us what mattered to the people. Most temples had friezes, but the decoration of the Parthenon was by far the most ambitious ever attempted by the Greeks.

The Parthenon Frieze, Phidias, about 438BC, 160 m in length, marble.

This continuous frieze ran right round the building. The backgrounds were painted bright blue and red. Metal ornaments were added and the rest was painted in bright colours. It must have shone with colour.

SCULPTURE FOR ALL

Not all sculpture was huge or made for public places. Some statuettes (mini statues) and small **reliefs** were made for people's homes. As well as stone (**marble**, **limestone** and **alabaster**) and metal (gold, silver, lead, **bronze** and iron), sculptors used ivory, bone, amber, wax, wood and especially **terracotta**.

Developing styles

Like the larger sculptures, these smaller sculptures show the same styles that developed through each period. Favourite subjects were human and animal figures. The sculptures were simply designed, but looked more relaxed and detailed by the **Classical** and **Hellenistic periods**. A lot of terracotta sculptures have been found in tombs. Many small sculptures were used as handles on vase lids.

Girls Playing, about 340BC, 14 cm, terracotta.

This statuette is of two girls playing the popular Greek game of knucklebones. Even though it is small, the poses are graceful and lifelike.

Colours of clay

Terracotta statuettes, like stone and wood, were painted brightly. **Archaic** statuettes of gods and goddesses were usually painted black, white, red and blue. Often these colourful creations had a more practical use as jugs or bottles.

Many later terracotta statuettes were little models of people doing everyday things such as kneading bread, looking after children, cutting wood or hair. By Hellenistic times, these statuettes were extremely popular. They are simple but charming. If you have ever tried making a clay model you will know how difficult such a statuette would be!

Painted wood or beeswax statuettes were also popular. The Greeks decorated their homes with little gods, goddesses and heroes or symbols of family life (mainly women and children). Statuette-making was big business!

Everyday things

Sculptors also made objects that people used in the home, such as toys, potties and cosmetic jars. Often these everyday things were buried with a person. Artists used as much artistic skill in these small household objects as they did for large statues. These terracotta feet from the 6th century BC are actually perfume bottles.

ANCIENT GREEK BUILDINGS

Buildings were designed to be as elegantly shaped as possible. Harmony and balance were most important to Greek **architects**. They created many splendid public buildings which have inspired architects throughout the ages. In fact the idea of building as an art form came from the Greeks. Another Greek idea is that each building's measurements are the key to its beauty.

Building design

Temples and palaces of **limestone** or **marble** were magnificent, but normal houses were built with sun-dried mud bricks. Roofs were tiled. The rooms were built around an open courtyard with windows facing inwards.

By about 400BC, open-air theatres were built. Seats were made of stone, cut into a hillside forming a kind of semicircle. The stage was low down in the centre.

The most important Greek buildings were temples. The first temples (built as homes for the gods) were built with wood. Their flat roofs were first supported on tree trunk pillars, then on rough columns of stone. From the 7th century BC, all public buildings, including temples, were made of limestone or marble.

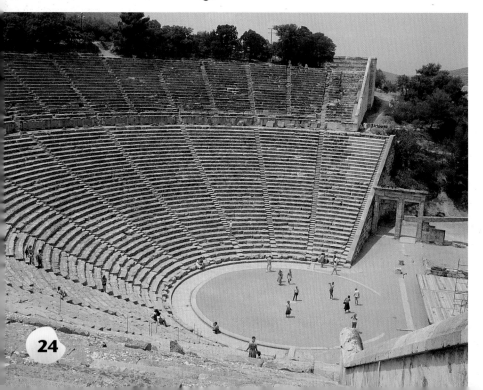

Greek theatre, Epidaurus, about 450BC, stone.

Greek theatres were brilliant examples of engineering and art. Cut into hillsides, they were designed so that everyone could see and hear everything that happened on stage.

Architectural styles

There were two main architectural styles in Greek temple building: the Doric and the Ionic. The Doric was popular in mainland Greece. Columns and capitals (the tops of columns) were plain. In eastern parts of Greece and the islands, the Ionic style was more common.

Columns were thinner and capitals were decorated with 'volutes' – swirls carved into the top four corners. Another style, Corinthian, had carvings in the shape of acanthus (a prickly plant) leaves on the capitals. The Greeks did not use the Corinthian style much, but the Romans loved it.

Erechtheion, Acropolis in Athens, 421–409BC, marble.

The Erechtheion is an Ionic temple built near to the Parthenon in Athens. It is famous for its fine proportions. In the porch, six statues of women took the place of columns, their hats holding up the capitals. Human-shaped columns like this are called caryatids.

RELIGIOUS BUILDINGS

Religious buildings, such as shrines and temples, were often the target of enemy soldiers when the city states were at war. When the Persians invaded in 490BC they also destroyed temples. The biggest of these was the **Acropolis**, a temple to Athena, in Athens. When the Persians were driven out in 479BC, the Athenians decided to rebuild the Acropolis. They also built an even more magnificent temple called the **Parthenon**.

Home for a goddess

The **architect** Ictinus designed and rebuilt the Parthenon between 447–438BC. This was the **Classical period**. The Parthenon was designed with such a sense of balance and harmony that it is still considered to be one of the greatest buildings ever constructed.

*The Parthenon, about 447–438BC, 70 x 30 m, **marble**.*

*Greek temples were open structures. The Parthenon rose up above Athens, a gleaming white columned monument. Measurements were worked out mathematically, giving the temple perfect **proportions**.*

How the Parthenon was built

The foundations were made from **limestone**, but the main building was in marble. Architects gave the stonemasons (stone cutters and carvers) instructions for precise block sizes and shapes which they cut using chisels and mallets. Finished blocks of stone were eased into place using ropes, pulleys and levers. Pieces of metal called cramps held them in place.

The columns were made to lean slightly inwards, drawing the eye upwards. The base of the temple curved at the centre to stop it looking as though it was sagging. Phidias, the sculptor, designed the **relief** carvings and the statues inside, but most were made by skilled craftsmen. The statue of Athena (on page 20) was heavily adorned with gold. It cost more than the Parthenon itself.

Beautiful buildings

Beauty and religion were important to the Greeks. By the Classical period, architects who designed religious buildings or monuments were valued highly.

Greek artists learned that our eyes can play tricks – straight lines do not always look straight. Using **optical illusions**, they could make buildings look striking and well balanced.

Temple of Athena Nike, about 425BC, marble.

Nike was the goddess of victory. This miniature Ionic style temple was built in the Acropolis after the Parthenon was completed.

THE SEARCH FOR BEAUTY

The Greeks' fascination with the mind and beauty brought the cleverest among them together. They discussed and criticized paintings, statues and buildings, inspiring artists to create even greater works.

Artists searched for beauty, harmony and a better understanding of people and the powers that control us. When they began experimenting, they introduced many new ideas about art to the world. Some of these ideas have lasted for centuries.

Useful evidence

The fact that Greek artists liked to show things as lifelike and realistic helps us to find out about the ancient Greeks. Studying their art shows us how important music and sport were to them. We can find out about their battles, armour and tactics. We can also discover details about their daily life. We know the sorts of things that happened at their parties. We know how they did their laundry. We know how they taught their children.

Greek inspirations

The ancient Greeks have influenced artists throughout history. The Romans were fascinated by them and copied much of their art, including their ideas and beliefs and writings, especially poems, plays and stories.

Nearly a thousand years later the Italians began to study the Greeks once more. This became a rebirth of thought and art and was later called the **Renaissance**.

Even today, throughout the world, many buildings resemble grand **Classical** temples. Paintings and statues are modelled on the Greeks' perfect **proportions** and balance. Pottery designs are inspired by their vases. The ancient Greeks gave us the idea that art means beauty. Artists have been affected by this idea ever since.

Woman Spinning, about 500BC, black and red paint on white-ground jug.

Some vases were coated with white paint and outline drawings in black and red paint added later. Women were often pictured on these vases, in graceful poses, often at their daily tasks. On this jug, a woman is spinning. In her left hand she holds a distaff which was a stick of wood or metal with a spike at one end and a handle at the other. It holds the ball of wool or flax. In her right hand, she spins the wool or flax into thread. This simple picture uses only the lines and colours necessary to give all that information in a balanced and clear way.

*Greek Woman, about 370BC, **marble**.*

Although she seems a bit stiff, see how lifelike this statue's hands look and how her clothes gently drape and fold. Soon, Greek sculptors produced even more lifelike work in relaxed and natural poses.

TIMELINE

BC

3000–1380	Crete, Minoan civilization.
2000–1000	Mycenaean civilization.
1100	The Geometric period begins.
776	The first Olympic Games held.
700	The Archaic period begins.
	Black-figure pottery is made in Athens.
640	The world's first roof tiles made at the Temple of Hera at Olympia.
about 550	The first plays are performed. The first coins made with writing on them.
520	Red-figure pottery is made in Athens.
500	The Classical Age begins.
490	Persians invade Greece, but are beaten at the Battle of Marathon.
480	Persians invade Greece, but are beaten at the Battle of Saramis.
479	The final Persian defeat on land at Palataea.
474	The building of the Parthenon begins in Athens.
467	The final Persian defeat at sea at Salamis.
450	Myron creates the Discobolus (the 'Discus Thrower').
438	Phidias creates the huge statue, Athena Parthenos.
432	The Parthenon is completed.
430	The Great Plague of Athens kills a quarter of all the people.
425	The Temple of Athena Nike is constructed.
336	Alexander the Great becomes ruler after his father, Philip, is murdered.
334	Alexander invades Asia.
329	Alexander reaches India.
323	The death of Alexander. His generals divide up his empire. The Hellenistic period begins.
320	The production of red-figure pottery in Athens ends.
179–168	The last Macedonian king, Philip, reigns.
147	The Romans destroy Corinth. Rome rules Greece and Macedonia directly.

GLOSSARY

acropolis a fortress on a hill where Greek citizens could go for safety

alabaster translucent (semi see-through) creamy-white stone

apprentices people learning a trade or craft by working with a skilled worker

Archaic period (700–500BC) when artists had to follow set rules when depicting objects and people

architect the word means 'master builder' in ancient Greek. Architects design and construct buildings.

black-figure style using red clay backgrounds artists painted black pictures and patterns

bronze hard-wearing brownish gold metal. A mixture of copper and tin.

Classical period (500–323BC) when artists showed a better understanding of proportion, weight and movement and art became more natural-looking

encaustic a method of painting using burnt wax

fresco a painting made on damp, freshly plastered walls

frieze a band or strip of decoration used to decorate a wall or piece of pottery

Geometric period (1100–700BC) when using lines and simple shapes were popular

Hellenistic period (323–100BC) when artists developed even more skills in showing natural forms and included flowing and magnificent details

limestone a creamy-white rock used for building and carving

marble a hard rock that comes in many colours. It can be polished to a high shine.

mural a painting made directly on the wall of a building. A fresco is a kind mural.

optical illusions appearances of things that tell your eyes something is there that is not really

parchment animal skin, scraped, dried and treated as a writing surface

Parthenon the largest temple in the Acropolis at Athens

pigment coloured powder made from plants, minerals or animals and mixed with various liquids to make paint

proportion measurements of different parts and how they look together

red-figure style from about 510BC, artists painted the background of their pottery black, leaving the figures unpainted so they appeared red

reliefs raised carved pictures

Renaissance a time of experiment in Europe when the skills of ancient Greece and Rome were studied and admired

symmetry the same on both sides

tempera paint in which the pigment (colour) is mixed with egg

terracotta means 'baked earth'. It is clay, usually a brownish-red and used to make pottery, tiles and statues.

INDEX

Numbers in plain type (24) refer to the text.
Numbers in bold type (**28**) refer to an illustration.